THE "H" WORD

THE "H" WORD

✦

The Cause of All Anger and Violence

Bernard R. Buetens, Ph.D.
Psychologist and Psychoanalytic
Psychotherapist

iUniverse, Inc.
New York Lincoln Shanghai

The "H" Word
THE CAUSE OF ALL ANGER AND VIOLENCE

iUniverse books may be ordered through booksellers or by contacting:

iUniverse
2021 Pine Lake Road, Suite 100
Lincoln, NE 68512
www.iuniverse.com
1-800-Authors (1-800-288-4677)

ISBN-13: 978-0-595-37916-3 (pbk)
ISBN-13: 978-0-595-82290-4 (ebk)
ISBN-10: 0-595-37916-8 (pbk)
ISBN-10: 0-595-82290-8 (ebk)

Printed in the United States of America

The author does not intend this book to be a substitute for advice from one's own medical or mental health professional who should be consulted before proceeding with any recommendations in The "H" Word.

Anyone with a known mental or serious health condition and/or taking prescription or non-prescription medication should seek professional medical advice before beginning or following the specific suggestions in behavioral changes.

Therefore, it is important that some people be in therapy or find a psychotherapist before proceeding with suggestions in this book. The author disclaims responsibility for any adverse effects arising from the use or application of the information contained in this book. It is possible that anger might serve as a defense or protection against more serious mental illness.

In any case, you should discuss all aspects of The "H" Word with your doctor or mental health professional as he or she might wish to suit the program to your specific needs.

This book is dedicated to my 103-year-young mother-in-law Kathleen Baer who is an inspiration to those who want to know how to live and enjoy life. She is an example of healthy narcissism, and during the many years of knowing her I have never seen her angry or speak badly of another person. She does not believe that it is "worth it" to be angry at things you have no power to change.

She has many grandchildren and great-grandchildren and is admired and adored by them all and by all who know her.

CONTENTS

ACKNOWLEDGMENTS

This book has been a family project, with joy and stress mixed in getting it completed. The idea and importance of humiliation is mine, but confirmed and affirmed by the rest of the family, along with all of my patients.

Thanks to my brother-in-law Eugene Baer for trying to make the book less academic and more readable. Thanks to my aunt Helen B. Rudman, an educator herself, for her encouragement and thoughts in completing the work. Also thanks to my other brother-in-law John W. Baer and his wife Mary, and to my wife and children who provided emotional support and helpful ideas.

I also want to give additional thanks to all of the principals, administrators, teachers of the "600" schools in New York City for their cooperation in my dissertation completed many years ago. They were truly dedicated heroes working under difficult conditions.

And also thanks to the many psychoanalysts who helped me learn how to do the work of psychoanalysis and psychotherapy.

Last but most important are my patients who provided the information which led to my discovery of the significance of over-sensitivity to embarrassment and humiliation.

INTRODUCTION

What is the "H" Word?

The title of this book <u>The "H" Word</u> does not refer to Hell or Heaven, but rather to the word *Humiliation.* Humiliation is a word that strikes fear into everyone. Who wants to be humiliated? We avoid humiliation like the plague. We have all experienced humiliation which is an intense emotion of feeling small, being destroyed or annihilated. People who are humiliated feel useless and powerless. There is only one natural response in return—anger. Wherever there is anger or violence you will find some form of humiliation. Unfortunately, the psychologists and social scientists of the world have neglected the association of anger and violence with humiliation. The hope of this book is to explain and understand the importance of humiliation in both a global world view and also as an individual problem.

I am in complete agreement with Thomas Friedman *The New York Times* columnist who wrote in 2003, "Humiliation is the single most underappreciated force in international relations".

I believe that the terrible state and condition of the world with its continuing aggression and violence needs desperate help to achieve peace. Aggression, violence and anger are the most difficult problems that psychologists, social scientists and politicians have to deal with. Just look at the violent chaotic state of the world today and since the beginning of time. Since I connect aggression and violence with humiliation, it is my hope that understanding the essence of humiliation will contribute to that goal of achieving peace.

As a psychologist and psychoanalyst, a professional who deals with individuals, my awareness of problems caused by humiliation has been a major breakthrough in dealing with my patients. Sigmund Freud, the father of modern psychology and psychiatry and founder of psychoanalysis, was himself unable to help one of his patients named Dora. This was a case he wrote about after his unsuccessful treatment. It is my opinion Freud failed to realize at the time that his style of therapy was causing anger. Humiliation or embarrassment made Dora withdraw from treatment before she was cured. It has been my experience that most cases of premature termination from therapy are the result of sensitivity to humiliation. Whenever a patient leaves before a cure, or whenever a patient becomes angry with the therapist, it is imperative that both the therapist and patient search for the underlying cause of humiliation or embarrassment. When these emotions are discussed and understood the treatment can resume.

This book is organized into five chapters. The first chapter explains the power of humiliation on a global and individual basis. The second chapter details how humiliation plays a comprehensive role in all aspects of life.
The third chapter deals with the psychology of humiliation. It contains technical information for therapists or patients or anyone who is interested in the psychology of humiliation. Chapter

four is devoted to methods of conquering humiliation. Chapter five is the summary and conclusion

This author has developed a new saying, "anything new is easier than you think and harder than you think". The trick is not to be intimidated at first and second to persevere even though it is difficult. My hope is that you will find this book easy to read, easy to follow, and in the end worth the effort.

1

THE POWER OF
THE "H" WORD

Humiliation is the raw material of anger and aggression. Many social scientists believe that anger and aggression are innate or inborn to the individual person, while other scientists believe that it is learned. I believe with many other scientists that aggression is a combination of innate and learning. While all people have muscles that can inflict damage by aggressive action, not everyone chooses to be violent. Anger and violence are learned early in life either unintentionally or intentionally and is the result of humiliations.

Hate Cultures:

A former psychoanalytic teacher of mine, Reuben Fine, a well-known and respected psychoanalyst and psychologist, wrote <u>The Meaning of Love in Human Experience</u> in which he describes most of the world as living in a hate culture. Only a few primitive people live in a love culture. Dr. Fine was looking for the cause of aggression in our culture and other cultures. Unfortunately, and like many other scientists before him, he was not aware of the importance of humiliation, which I consider to be the basis of all violence, anger and destruction.

Nevertheless, the following is a summary of what Dr. Fine found in the hate cultures: "(1). a general atmosphere of hatred, violence and discord with an ever present fear of death. (2). if there is any love present, it is limited to the family or tribe and is a rarely reliable. (3). the desire for vengeance is omni-present. (4). reliance on magic and sorcery is widespread. (5). sex is for conquest with little or no affection. (6). women are devalued and children are of little consequence. (7). life for the members of these cultures is miserable in the extreme. (8). revenge dominates. (9). individual differences can be found in each culture." My belief is that all these hate cultures have a common factor of humiliation, which leads to anger and violence. Reuben Fine did not use the word humiliation but believed that only education and psychotherapy could transform the society of nations into a love culture.

Love Cultures:

In contrast to the hate cultures, Dr. Fine's summary of love cultures is as follows: "(1). love cultures stress love, affection, tenderness and cooperation (2).the major characteristic of love cultures is the general feeling of harmony that is absent in the hate cultures (3).that aggression is universal, but what differentiates love and hate cultures is the absence of hostility, worry, unlimited violence, warfare, fighting and murder (4).love cultures allow wide latitude of sexual expression (5).in general, persons living in the love cultures are fairly happy and contented with their lives; severe emotional conflict and mental disorders are rare (6).in general, the descriptions apply to the majority of people, but not to everyone in the group."

The contrast between hate cultures and love cultures is very dramatic. We can see that in hate cultures and all societies that live with humiliation and violence can be considered psychotic, because they care little for human life and avoid reality. We may now ask how hate cultures develop.

How Hate Develops:

My idea is that anger and hate are learned from the environment, mainly from parents or significant family members. This anger and the following violence develop from humiliations. For instance, in our present day culture, we learn anger and violence by experiencing humiliation at the hands of parents, parent surrogates, family members and unsophisticated teachers. Every person without exception has experienced humiliation in some form. When a young child does something his parents disapprove of and the parents say "No", the child will often feel humiliated and angry. How many people while growing up and expressing some anger at another person, such as a sibling, have heard the comment from parents "shush" or "what will the neighbors think?" or other words to that effect. This type of comment from the parents can have a strong effect on a child and lead to inhibitions or even more serious conditions such as physical or mental illness. By these remarks the child can interpret that the neighbors or others are more important than they are. Thus early in life we are told to keep our emotions under control or suppressed. Some children can do this without symptoms or distress because of sufficient love or caring, but many children can be harmed. When the love of the child by the parent overrides humiliation, emotional development can proceed normally. If the humiliation is too severe, the mental and emotional development of the child will become distorted and can lead to various types of emotional and physical problems, such as stunted emotional and physical growth. Symptoms can be headaches, stomachaches and other problems. The child may also learn how to humiliate others and/or become angry, violent and aggressive.

Specifically, parents' sensitivity to humiliation is easily spread to children, because the parents as children were humiliated by their parents and so on. The power of humiliation is fed by unconscious or unaware pleasure in humiliating others. When a person gets pleasure in humiliating others, he or she is also sensitive to humiliation and fears being humiliated. One reduces his own fear of humiliation by humiliating others. In addition, this fear will hamper emotional growth and thus is the basis for all phobias.

Reversing the Damage:

Even though anger and violence are learned from the environment, this damage can be reversed in two ways. First, there must be early intervention in child development. For example, parents should learn to reduce their criticism of their children and stop their own behavior that tries to embarrass or humiliate the child. Instead parents can ask the child "Is there a better way to behave"? Or "What have I done to cause you to act this way"? Second, parents can teach by example better ways of expressing emotions instead of reacting with anger and violence. Third, the destructive continuous link from grandparents to parents and children in regards to humiliation and embarrassment must be broken. The humiliation and embarrassment of children can be reduced by the parents becoming aware of the unconscious and conscious pleasure they receive from trying to humiliate their children.

Health Problems:

In addition, the power of humiliation can also cause severe health problems. There is evidence that coronary disease is caused by anger. In a 1996 *Harvard Health Letter*" Taking Emotions to Heart", Leah R. Garnett discussed emotions and the heart. Essentially the author said that anger kills because it causes heart disease. She then described in detail numerous studies of how this happens. In a May 2004 article in the *American Family Physician*, "Negative Emotions Increase Coronary Heart Disease Risk," written by Richard Sadovsky, M.D, explained how depression, anxiety and other negative emotions are associated with increased risk for coronary heart disease. There are a multitude of articles on the internet that connect anger with physical and mental illness. However, no one until now has put anger and humiliation together to make an important syndrome that needs attention and repair.

A Personal Experience:

The following is a personal experience illustrating the power of humiliation. I was a school psychologist in the 1960s and 1970s and assigned to schools for emotionally disturbed boys. In New York City these schools were called "600 schools" because their numbers were listed in the 600's (611, 612 and so forth). There were less than a dozen of these schools. The pupils were adolescent boys who could not remain in regular schools because of their disruptive or aggressive behavior. In the 600 schools attempts were made to correct their behavior, but it was a difficult task. The students responded to teachers they were afraid of, and the teachers who showed the most anger were the most successful in suppressing the angry outbursts in the classroom. But as soon as the students were released from the custody of teachers they feared, they were again on the warpath with vengeance. The students provoked each other with remarks meant to humiliate, with many of these remarks directed at their target's mother. These remarks were quickly followed by physical reactions, which sooner or later led to teacher involvement. Although the schools seemed to be in a state of impending turmoil, each year they had interesting and excellent graduation exercises which were all praise and no humiliation. The administrators and teachers were truly heroes in the difficult work they were doing.

Change from Frustration to Humiliation:

In addition to working in the "600 Schools," I was also working towards my Ph.D. For my thesis I wrote a paper comparing these students' behavior with so-called normal students in a regular junior high. The title of my thesis was *The Comparative Effects of Affection and Hostility in Reducing of Frustration Induced Anger among Delinquent and Non-Delinquents*. As the title suggests, I studied the effect of frustration on delinquent and non-delinquents. Based on the work of Dollard and Miller (1939), it was then widely believed that frustration was the cause of aggression. I now have ample reason to believe that frustration is not the main cause of anger and aggression, it is a symptom. Frustration leads to humiliation. In addition, the change in my thinking that anger comes from humiliation instead of frustration developed from my work and experience with some private patients who became angry during therapy. I discovered that the analytic work in itself was humiliating and causing anger, instead of frustration causing anger. The discovery that any frustration the patients felt was caused by humiliation or embarrassment made a large difference in my treatment method.

Sensitivity to Humiliation and Embarrassment:

Furthermore, it was not just humiliation itself that was causing the anger. The amount of sensitivity to these emotions (humiliation and embarrassment or shame) experienced by the patients was the culprit. Everyone feels humiliation and the other emotions, but the degree of sensitivity to them causes anger. I now have discovered methods to reduce the degree of sensitivity to humiliation and embarrassment. This will be discussed in detail in Chapter 4.

If I had been aware in the past of the importance for dealing with sensitivity to humiliation, the delinquent boys in the "600" Schools would have been helped more to reduce their sensitivity to anger and aggression. Let's face it—everyone experiences humiliation. It is an intense emotion of feeling destroyed, small, useless and powerless, in other words a loss of control. The natural response is anger which can lead to violence against oneself or others. Wherever there is anger or violence, you will find some form of humiliation.

Thus, in over thirty years experience as a psychologist and psychoanalyst, I have found that developing an awareness of humiliation in both myself and patients has been a major therapeutic tool. Humiliation is a powerful force that exists in all aspects of life: personal, global, business, education, and social—the list is endless. We see it in the driver on the road who experiences road rage, the bully in the schoolyard, and the boss from hell. All are examples of the power of humiliation. Everyone is vulnerable to humiliation. However, some people are more sensitive to it than others.

Suicide and Humiliation:

Moreover, because there are millions of people in the world who are too sensitive to humiliation, they live in a constant state of humiliation, feeling annihilated, as if they don't exist. This is a painful state that can lead to suicide. It is my assessment that anyone who commits suicides is suffering from such a high state of humiliation and, thus, must try to end the suffering. Anger can lead to extreme violence either against oneself or others.

Even though humiliation is powerful, people the world over can reduce their "sensitivity" or fear of humiliation. It is possible to understand yourself better, especially as to why you get angry and why you often feel humiliated.

2

HUMILIATION IN
EVERYDAY LIFE

In this chapter I will discuss how humiliation is part of everyday life and is seen in many different situations or conditions. It is a ubiquitous part of the human condition, and no one can avoid it. Included is information about relationships, depression, aging, writing and creativity, performance anxiety, a personal experience, emotion, education, string theory, face validity, comedy, criminality, road rage and the human condition.

Relationships:

From my experience as a psychologist and psychoanalyst I have concluded that the main cause of problems with couples is over-sensitivity to humiliation. These troubles cause anger that is difficult to reduce because the humiliation is directed to the people we hope to love and be loved by. Our sensitivity to humiliation also causes each party to be on the alert for criticism and increases distance instead of emotional closeness.

Furthermore, at the start of a new relationship each person views the other as being separate from the past and therefore with fewer problems in the new relationship. With the passing of time and getting to know each other, the memory of the earlier relationships with the parents of the past reappears.

These reminders of the past can be good or bad depending on how the relationships with the parents have been. If the parents enjoyed humiliating their children, these emotions will be passed on to the children who will then try to humiliate their partners. This repetition from the past and its disruptive impact in the present is a major cause of marital breakups. Based on the above description, the first sign or symptom of trouble is lack of sexual interest. In order to have a good relationship each partner has to make changes that include emotional separation from parents. They must not allow old parental problems to be repeated in the present relationship. The most important change must include a reduction in the sensitivity to humiliation. This will increase trust of the partner.

Also, those in a relationship have mental images of themselves and of their partners. To the extent that these mental pictures are healthy, so too will be the mental health of the couple. If these mental pictures of self and other are with love, the person will function well and be happy. If the mental pictures are fragmented with fears and anxiety, which comes about by fear of humiliation, unhappiness follows and poor mental health occurs.

Depression:

In addition to relationship problems, another clue to humiliation in your life is the painful condition of depression. The American Heritage Dictionary defines depression as: "(1) the condition of feeling sad or despondent, and (2) a psychotic disorder characterized by an inability to concentrate, insomnia, loss of appetite, anhedonia, and feeling of extreme sadness, guilt, helplessness and hopelessness, and thoughts of death". When people become angry with themselves for reasons either conscious or unconscious and cannot shift the blame to others, the anger is directed at the self. This self-directed anger is most likely caused by unconscious feelings of humiliation or shame of which the individual is not aware. In psychotherapy if my patient discusses feelings of depression, we first search together for the underlying anger. Since humiliation and anger go hand in hand, the patient suffers from depression. When the cause of the humiliation is found, the anger and depression are usually reduced or eliminated.

Therefore, I believe depression is anger from humiliation turned inward. When people become angry with themselves—for reasons either conscious or unconscious—the blame and anger becomes internalized (brought inside the person). These people are not able to shift the blame to others. This may come from early experiences with parents who have taught their children to suppress angry feeling towards others. Instead of recognizing the source of anger and humiliation, the anger is directed at the self.

<u>Aging:</u>

Another example of humiliation in life is fear of aging. Many dollars are spent trying to remain young. The use of cosmetics and creams, along with surgery and health spas, are geared to keep one looking young. Why are we so passionate about this?

Is it to prevent the humiliation of aging? Many people want to avoid looking old, because it causes them either embarrassment or humiliation. The normal and usual behavior is to compare the way one looked in the past to the reality of today. Also there is an unrealistic attempt to compare oneself to young people. It can become an obsession to look and feel more attractive and more loved.

That is to say, that looking old is felt as either embarrassment or humiliation. Nevertheless, one must accept reality. Aging is a normal part of living. What makes aging so fearful? The answer is that this is the ultimate humiliation—death. Again, we are facing annihilation. Being truly annihilated is the ultimate humiliation. However, the less one is sensitive to humiliation, the easier it becomes to accept reality. This includes aging and death.

Moreover, it is important to reduce sensitivity to humiliation in aging in order to live a normal and productive life. One must accept that aging is a part of living. What makes humiliation so feared is its connection to the fear of death. The thought that one will no longer exist, or be annihilated, is understandably humiliating. However, the less one is sensitive to humiliation the easier it will be to accept.

Writing and Creativity:

In addition, humiliation can also interfere with many areas of life. For instance, in order to write or produce any work of art, the author or artist must reduce any possible over-sensitivity to humiliation. Why is this so? Anything that is presented to the public will invite criticism, and in order to continue with any work the artist or writer must be able to overcome fear of embarrassment or humiliation.

Performance Anxiety:

Also, over-sensitivity to humiliation is related to one special type of anxiety known as performance anxiety. If you are afraid of making a fool of yourself this can translate into fear of being humiliated or embarrassed. Humiliation means being annihilated or no longer alive. In the unconscious (the deepest layer of the psyche) the experience of humiliation means being small or no longer existing.

Thus, a person trained to be a performer (actor or even politician) must get over this fear of performing in public. One often hears how some professionals undergo intense anxiety before a performance, yet when the time comes they still do a credible job. However, the wear and tear on psyche and body will always exist unless he learns to overcome the fear of this emotion. I tell some patients who are actors that they must reduce their sensitivity to humiliation in order to enjoy their work. Once this is achieved one can feel good about doing a satisfying job in the profession. Also in order to feel joy and happiness about one's achievement it is necessary to reduce sensitivity to humiliation.

In addition, this fear of performing also applies to all of us who are overly anxious about having to make a speech or appear before an audience, either for work or social reasons. Once again, reducing fear or over-sensitivity to humiliation is the key to allowing us not only to perform in public, but also to enjoy the process.

Personal Experience:

In other words, humiliation, fear of humiliation and over-sensitivity to humiliation affect us all. The recognition of humiliation as an essential idea or concept came to me through three paths. The first was my work as a psychologist in the 600 schools. The second was my experience in my own psychoanalysis. The third was my work with patients.

As mentioned earlier, I was a New York City School Psychologist in the 1960s and 1970s assigned to schools for emotionally disturbed boys. The schools were for adolescent boys who could not remain in regular classrooms because of disruptive behavior. Many different attempts including psychotherapy were tried to improve behavior, but each was only partially successful. In fact, the boys only seemed to respond to teachers that they feared. It was frustrating not to be able to help the students reduce their anger although much effort was extended by the mental health staff. At that time I was aware of the importance of anger but not to anger's relationship to sensitivity to humiliation.

Furthermore, in my own psychoanalysis I had learned the importance of sensitivity to anxiety. Although sensitivity to anxiety is important, it is not as vital as other emotions such as embarrassment, shame and humiliation. Indeed, I now think that it is really humiliation or the fear thereof that is the major cause of anxiety.

As time went on, I gradually increased my private practice and began working exclusively with neurotic or what I call "relatively healthy" patients. These are mainly individuals who are bothered by feelings that inhibit their freedom to be themselves and succeed, either personally, professionally, or both. These patients have everyday problems of not reaching their potential and other discomfits. However, they are not content to accept this. These patients want to change the way they live professionally, personally or both, and although they may be sensitive to humiliation, it has not stopped them from wanting to grow emotionally. In contrast to these healthy patients, the main reason most people with problems avoid getting professional help is because of their fear of being humiliated.

Therefore, when treating patients today, I now focus on reducing over-sensitivity to humiliation instead of concentrating on anxiety. I have found that anxiety is not the underlying cause of a patient's hesitancy to talk. Rather, it is a symptom. Fear of being humiliated leads to anxiety. Anxiety, therefore, is another result of the underlying fear of sensitivity to humiliation.

<u>Emotions:</u>

Another important feature of conventional therapy that contributes to mental health is the understanding of emotions. In a book called <u>Emotional Intelligence</u> by Daniel Goleman, a former science reporter for *The New York Times,* the importance of emotions was emphasized and brought to the attention of the public. Before this book, it was mainly IQ or Intelligence Quotient that was considered important when referring to success in life.

However, Goleman's book is technical and not easy for the average reader to understand because of its complexity. As complicated and as complete as this book is, Goleman left out what I believe is the most important emotion that exists—humiliation. He does include the emotion of anger and anger reduction, but he makes no connection between anger and humiliation, which is the main point of my book. By omitting the emotion of humiliation, Goleman's book is deficient. I believe that the foundations of anger and many other uncomfortable emotions are caused by either humiliation or the fear of humiliation. I have also developed the concept of over-sensitivity to humiliation, embarrassment and shame.

Although Goleman is correct in asserting that emotions and emotional intelligence are important for everyone who wants to function well, he does not recognize that without facing up to humiliation or the fear of humiliation one cannot reach emotional intelligence. Without understanding humiliation one cannot deal with anger. Anger can lead to destructive rage. In order to have emotional intelligence one must understand the importance of humiliation and how to deal with it. If a person can be aware that anger is generated by humiliation and learns what can be done about it, then emotional intelligence is achieved. When emotions are then better understood, this could have a major impact on the mental health of not only the self, but globally.

<u>Education:</u>

Another aspect of humiliation in everyday life in addition to emotional intelligence is education. Education has been suggested as contributing to mental health. There are two types of educational processes: direct and indirect. The first method is traditional whereby a teacher informs the students the information they need to know. The second method is subtler, where the teacher takes a more passive role and allows the students to learn at their own rate. Here the teacher steps in only when necessary and is more supportive and less critical than in the direct method.

Therefore, in the psychotherapy process, the education should be the second type—indirect. In the sessions, the patients talk about themselves and when they get stuck or speechless the therapist steps in and help the patient to continue talking. This leads to education about the self and how to improve.
I believe that the area most important is learning about situations that cause anger.

When the therapist or teacher helps the patient or student understand that the cause of anger comes from humiliation and helps trace the reasons for the humiliation, the anger disappears. This indirect learning can be beneficial to the individual's personality and their relationships with other people.

One personal example of education and humiliation comes from an experience with a patient, Ms. Y, who was going to medical school. I told her that medical school professors are known for their proclivity to try to humiliate their students.

This also applies to law school professors as described in a book <u>One L: the Turbulent True Story of a First Year at Harvard Law School</u> by Scott Turow.

I told Ms. Y not to take being humiliated personally because it was a typical process that gives the professors a great deal of pleasure. This is how the doctors themselves were trained, and they repeat the process. By not taking it personally, the student (my patient) was able to accept the criticisms objectively instead of subjectively and breezed through the program with honors.

Furthermore, when working with my patients, I encourage them not to respond angrily to others who do not agree with them. I also recommend to all teachers if they want to be successful with their students, the less humiliation the better. Instead of telling the students "they are wrong," the corrections can be made more tolerable by asking for "other possibilities?" Being aware of the negative effects of humiliation on students by teachers can go a long way in achieving success.

Comparison to String Theory:

The importance of humiliation as a social theory can be compared with physics String Theory. In the physics of String Theory an attempt is made by physical scientists to unify the three known forces, gravity, electromagnetism and quantum theory. In a similar fashion, if all the important emotions were understood, <u>The "H" Word</u> theory could lead to a unified social theory, and we would be able to reduce the major cause of hatred and instruction. We can do this by putting humiliation forward as the major cause of hatred and destruction keeping people apart. The opposite pole, love, brings people together. This can be called the unified social theory. This theory can explain almost all human behavior because the two main instinctual drives are love and hate. The reason people hate and destroy their fellow human beings is caused by conscious or unconscious humiliation as a major underlying emotion. I believe all mental illness is based on humiliation, either during early development or later by cultural, economic or other social forces. Humiliation causes severe reactions in people that can lead to suicide and even taking others along with them. Only the mentally healthy can love. This can be accomplished by reducing over-sensitivity to humiliation to a minimum. If we can get to the underlying cause of all mental illness, which I have discovered is humiliation, the unification of social theory can be realized.

Face Validity:

One may ask what makes me think that humiliation causes anger. What is the evidence? The evidence is that humiliation is a major part of everyone's life. Whether or not a person actually becomes humiliated, the fear of this emotion can be with us constantly. If this fear is too extensive or too intensive to a person, it can be debilitating and caused inhibition in functioning. The results can be chaos or disaster. This can be seen in one's personal life. Frustration, criticism, name-calling, and road rage, for example, are fundamental forms of humiliation. If you look back and trace all the times you have been angry, you will trace it back to some form of humiliation. In technical language this is called "face validity." It is obvious just by looking at it. Try it! Look at the last time you were angry. What do you think caused it or who? Remember, anger and humiliation goes together. Conquer one and you have conquered the other.

Comedy and Humiliation:

Another aspect or turnabout in humiliation is that the very people most sensitive to it are probably the people who get the most pleasure trying to humiliate others. For example, most comedy is based on humiliation. Comedians such as Johnny Carson, Jay Leno, Jon Stewart, David Letterman, and the entire group of comics are funny because they humiliate their guests and then allow the guests to retaliate. The well-known television program "Seinfeld" is based on humiliation. The show consists of the four main characters, Kramer, George, Elaine and Jerry who constantly humiliate each other either by direct confrontation or friendly attacks.

Criminality and Humiliation:

In contrast to comedians using humiliation, there is a more serious or pathological (mental illness) direction. For example, criminals break the law and take chances of incarceration that promise humiliation. Why do they take the chance of being so punished? Some of these criminal types are masochistic in the sense that they have unconscious wishes to be caught and sent away, because of their unconscious pleasure in being humiliated or other unknown reasons. This behavior usually comes about by experiences in early life where there was too much humiliation by important people, such as parents or surrogates.

Road Rage:

When a driver of a car is cut off by another driver or receives an obscene gesture and then tries to get even, what is known as road rage becomes a stimulus for destructive behavior. This angry behavior is caused by humiliation.

In 2006, *The Associated Press* released an article entitled "Road Rage Gets a Medical Diagnosis"—"Intermittent Explosive Disorder." This affects millions according to a US survey. The definition of "Intermittent Explosive Disorder" is "…multiple outbursts that are way out of proportion to the situation, and include threats or aggressive actions and property damage." The study of this disorder was based on a survey of 9,282 US adults who answered a diagnostic questionnaire and was funded by the National Institute of Mental Health. It was also found that the disorder was much more common than previously thought, and the finding was a surprise to the mental health specialists.

Psychiatrists think that the disorder is caused by inadequate production of serotonin—a mood regulator and behavior— inhibiting brain chemical. They believe that treatment with antidepressants along with behavior therapy akin to anger management is helpful. The findings also confirm that for most people, the difficulties of the disorder started during childhood or adolescence and often have an important effect on a person's life.

Notwithstanding the above findings, I consider this disorder to be part of the package of over-sensitivity to humiliation which probably came from early environmental influences and leads to anger and violence. The study on road rage indicates how prevalent road rage symptoms exist.

Human Condition:

Because over-sensitivity to humiliation is part of the "human condition," everyone has it to some degree. Humiliation affects each person differently, but with the same negative results if not dealt with correctly. Fear of humiliation is the main source of frustration, anger, and panic or anxiety attacks.

Example of Humiliation in Everyday Life:

Similarly, it is easy to see how any treatment procedure can result in embarrassment and humiliation. For example, this is not unlike the humiliation that occurs in a hospital when a patient is told to put on a flimsy robe so that they can be examined. In the movie "The Doctor," William Hurt a well-respected but pompous physician becomes a patient. He then gets insight as to the patient's humiliation. When a patient is reassured that the attending physician cares about embarrassment or humiliation, this can lead to a marked improvement in cooperation between patient and the doctor.

3

PSYCHOLOGY AND HUMILIATION

This chapter has two main categories: Theory and Practice. The first part of this chapter will discuss the psychological and psychoanalytic theory pertaining to humiliation. The second part will discuss the practice and therapy relating to the emotions of humiliation, embarrassment and shame.

THEORY

Insufficient Appreciation of Humiliation:

Even though it could be argued that humiliation and its cousin embarrassment have already been studied in the psychology field, I believe it has not been fully appreciated. Instead, these emotions have been identified as a certain type of personalities called "Narcissistic Personality Disorder." By keeping humiliation limited to narcissism the importance of these emotions are restricted. Could it be that the reason for this insufficient recognition of humiliation is that the very people who are trained to help, that is, psychiatrists, psychologists, psychoanalysts and social workers, are themselves over-sensitive to humiliation and therefore avoid dealing with it. Even the illustrious father of psychoanalysis, Sigmund Freud, ignored or did not understand its importance.

Embarrassment:

In addition to humiliation, another important emotion is embarrassment. My idea is to separate humiliation and embarrassment. I link libido and sexual feelings to embarrassment, while humiliation is associated with anger and aggression. Strong emotions such as over-sensitivity to humiliation and embarrassment can interfere with people's functioning and satisfactions in life. Having a relationship with a suitable partner is important to enjoying life. It is difficult to have an amiable relationship with a partner if one or the other is over-sensitive to humiliation or embarrassment. The normal everyday clashes require that partners be able to overlook differences in opinions and personality traits so that harmony can exist. This can only happen when a person reduces over-sensitivity to humiliation and embarrassment.

Definitions:

As mentioned earlier, there is little recognition of humiliation. Psychoanalytic Terms and Concepts of the American Psychoanalytic Association is the book considered to be the standard reference book for American practitioners of psychoanalysis. However, even here there is no definition or recognition for the term humiliation.

Yet, there is a definition for shame. Quoting from the above book, "...shame refers to a broad spectrum of painful affects—embarrassment, humiliation, mortification, disgrace—that accompany the feelings of being rejected, ridiculed, exposed, while losing the respect of others. Early experiences of being seen, looked at, exposed, and scorned are significant in producing shame."

Also, in this psychoanalytic dictionary there is no difference in definitions of shame, embarrassment and humiliation. Therefore, I am **originating a new concept** to the psychoanalytic literature whereby **shame and embarrassment** are related to **libido (sex)** and **humiliation** is related to **anger and aggression.** In my opinion, when working with patients it is important to differentiate between shame and humiliation. Of the two, humiliation's aggressive intent is a more difficult emotion to deal with than shame.

Another definition of shame in The New Heritage Dictionary is as follows: "1. a painful emotion caused by a strong sense of guilt, embarrassment, unworthiness, or disgrace. 2. one that brings dishonor or disgrace on. 3. a condition of disgrace or dishonor; ignominy."

Also, the New Heritage Dictionary definition of embarrass is as follows: "…to cause to feel self-conscious or ill at ease: disconcert: (meeting adults embarrasses the shy child)."

Furthermore, the definition of humiliate in the same New Heritage Dictionary is as follows: "…to lower the pride, dignity, self respect of. To Degrade. To Humble."

Moreover, in the <u>English Dictionary,</u> definitions of the three important words shame, embarrass and humiliate are the same and disregard any difference and meanings. Again, I maintain the difference in meanings by using aggression and destruction for humiliation and libidinal or sexual ideas for shame and embarrassment. My definitions also include combinations and mixing of the emotions of shame, embarrassment and humiliation. For example, there can be aggressive sex which is humiliation plus embarrassment.

Definition of Sensitivity:

Throughout this book I use the word "sensitivity." This usually appears with "sensitivity to humiliation" and other emotions such as "anxiety or shame". <u>The New Heritage Dictionary's</u> definition for "sensitivity" is as follows: "…the quality or condition of being sensitive; the capacity of an organ or organism to respond to stimulation."

The definition of sensitivity to anxiety as defined in the book <u>Psychoanalytic Terms and Concepts</u> is "…the unpleasurable affect or emotional state characterized by feelings of unpleasant anticipation—a sense of imminent danger". An example of sensitivity to anxiety comes from my own psychoanalysis. At the beginning of my treatment, I had trouble finding what to talk about. My analyst interpreted that the difficulty in talking was anxiety. It was suggested that I reduce my "over-sensitivity" to anxiety. This would allow me to speak more easily. With effort and practice I was able to accomplish this, and the analysis continued with fewer interruptions.

Therefore, using my own experience as the background for this book, I am now applying reducing over-sensitivity to humiliation and anger as I learned to do with anxiety. However, I have discovered that anxiety was not really the issue; in my own treatment it was a result of my own sensitivity to humiliation.

Definition of Anxiety :

According to the American Psychoanalytic Association's Psychoanalytic Terms and Concepts, anxiety is "an unpleasurable affect or emotional state characterized by feelings of unpleasant anticipation—a sense of imminent danger. Its intensity and duration vary considerably. Anxiety has both physiological and psychological correlates; common physiological manifestations are acceleration of heart and breathing rates, tremor, sweating, diarrhea, and muscle tension. Anxiety, which is related to a danger that is unconscious, should be distinguished from fear, which is a response to a consciously recognized external and realistic danger".

Levels of Anxiety:

I consider humiliation to be basic to feelings of unhappiness and neurosis (distortions in thinking) and is connected to the professionally accepted psychoanalytic levels of anxiety. In psychoanalytic theory, there are five levels of anxiety. The five levels of anxiety are: (1) fear of annihilation, (2) fear of loss of the loved person, (3) fear of loss of love, (4) fear of bodily harm or injury known as castration anxiety, and (5) fear of criticism of the conscience, known as the superego.

Furthermore, the most intense of these anxieties is the fear of annihilation, which means a person no longer exists or is destroyed. My discovery is that fear of annihilation is the same dread that pertains to humiliation.

Thus, in these five levels of anxiety, the most dreaded and deepest level is annihilation. Therefore, I have discovered that fear of annihilation is really the fear of humiliation. I believe that all types of anxiety touch upon the fear of annihilation. The level above annihilation is fear of loss of an important person. This causes panic because the feeling not only applies to the loss of an important person but to fear of annihilation or humiliation. Again, all types of anxiety are related to humiliation.

The next level of anxiety above fear of loss of important person is a fear of *loss of love* from the important person. This is also painful, but not as strong as lower levels. Again, the discomfort dips into the lower levels and wherever there is anxiety there is some fear of humiliation. A healthy person with good defenses can avoid discomfort to a large extent.

Similarly, according to Sigmund Freud and accepted psychoanalytic theory, the next higher level of anxiety is fear of physical injury. People who are always afraid of losing their health are usually fixated at this level of anxiety. All discomfort levels are based on the person's developmental and emotional background. For example, if you had five levels of a parking garage, the lowest level of the garage would be annihilation, the next higher level of the garage or level number four would be fear of loss of an important person and so forth. When a person had a reduced level of lower anxieties, the higher levels are much easier to deal with and have a smaller effect on discomfort.

Likewise, the level above health anxiety is considered to be the fear of one's conscience or Superego. The higher the person's level of emotional development, the probability will be of a higher functioning conscience or Superego. If the earlier development has been unstable, the shakier will be the conscience. This means that a part of the person's personality called the conscience will either be too strict or to loose. This can cause a person to be either too rigid or inflexible—or can lead to criminality or other sociopath pathologies. It is important to have the correct balance in conscience functioning in order to be a happy effective person.

<u>Signal Anxiety:</u>

However, no one can get through life without some anxiety. A healthy person deals with what is known as "signal anxiety." This means that a "signal of anxiety" reaches the person and can put into effect some type of defense that will prevent the anxiety from being more intense. It happens quickly and most people are unaware when this signal is happening. An example is when one needs to do something uncomfortable, such as asking the boss for a raise. Instead of feeling anxiety, the person might rationalize that the raise in pay is not really needed and not ask for the raise. The other alternative is to comfortably learn how to explain to the boss why the raise is deserved.

Signal Anger:

Furthermore, in addition to signal anxiety I have discovered an important adjunct to mental health that I call *"signal anger"*. Anyone who experiences anger should be made aware of these feelings and then trace the humiliation responsible for this anger. When one finds the cause of anger, the humiliation will diminish. The ability to do this will lead to a reduction in over-sensitivity to humiliation and to better and stable mental health.

Psychopaths and Sociopaths:

Thus, in this book the "H" Word is for people with everyday normal problems. It is not for persons who are psychopaths or sociopaths, because they already have too little conscience. That means that these people are already not sensitive to humiliation and do not need any additional help in reducing humiliation sensitivity. Instead, they need help in increasing sensitivity to humiliation or else they are beyond help in leading a normal life. Psychopaths and sociopaths do not have a conscience or Superego to deter them from acting or taking actions that might instigate humiliation such as incarceration. They do not care about such emotions and can take chances that the average per-son would avoid.

Narcissistic Rage:

So far I have described how sensitivity to humiliation results in anger and aggression. In the psychoanalytic literature, anger is described as narcissistic rage or injury. This means rage resulting from damage to the self-image or self-esteem. My dispute with the present day literature is to the theory that narcissistic rage is limited to people who have what is known as a "Narcissistic Personality Disorder". This is a mental condition where other people are not important. My contention is that everyone is sensitive to narcissistic injury more or less. The difference in personalities is the amount of sensitivity to humiliation each person can tolerate. The variations are not wide except in certain categories of personality such as psychopath or sociopath. The basic diagnosis of Neurosis (distortions of reality) would put most people in the category of over-sensitive to humiliation.

There is insufficient attention and lack of information in the psychoanalytic literature to the importance of humiliation. I have found it helpful to deal with over-sensitivity to humiliation in patients who have transferred from previous therapists, because anger was not dealt with properly in their previous treatment. Also, my supervisees who are themselves psychoanalysts have been using this new procedure of interpreting over-sensitivity to humiliation in their work and report excellent results.

Infantile Narcissism:

In addition, my thinking on "over-sensitivity to humiliation" is based on the left over remnants of infantile narcissism that all people go through. Infantile narcissism is a phase in early childhood where everything is expected to be given to us and if not we cry and scream. Parents usually try to supply the needs of the child—either for food or comfort in closeness. If there is too much or too little nurturance, the results can lead to some form of pathology or mental illness. However, the proper balance is not easy to achieve. When the parents are not successful in this nurturance, the grown child and now adult will maintain his need for total entitlement. This entitlement is based on magical thinking or distortions in the unconscious. Most people have leftover needs for infantile narcissism and are over-sensitive to humiliation and embarrassment. This can be observed in people who are easily angered. Wherever there is oversensitivity to humiliation or embarrassment, you will find either overt or covert anger.

Infantile Narcissism in an Adult:

Thus, infantile narcissism is necessary for life when a person is an infant or a child. When this narcissism is extreme and carried into adulthood, it is pathological. This leads to magical thinking that interferes with reality. Pathological narcissism results in ease of anger and poor relationships with people. Even worse, it can be turned against the self and lead to depression. If the feeling of entitlement is not fulfilled, the depressed person can become mentally ill. This leads to extreme forms of aggression including suicide or murder. While there is a narcissistic (self-love) element in all healthy people, when self-love is assaulted it becomes uncomfortable. Therefore, any humiliation is experienced as an attack on this narcissism. People will do anything, conscious or unconscious, to avoid the possibility of an attack on their narcissism to avoid humiliation. This is not a new idea, but what is different is my emphasis on the importance of humiliation as an attack on everyone's narcissism.

Narcissistic Personality Disorder:

However, you do not have to be neurotic or have a "Narcissistic Personality Disorder" to have over-sensitivity to humiliation or embarrassment. The therapy profession believes that the diagnosis of Narcissistic Personality Disorder refers to those persons who respond with violence or anger to a provocation caused by humiliation. Some people are simply more over-sensitive to humiliation than others. Personality types such as severe narcissists are either immune to humiliation or have such strong defenses or protection from this emotion that they function without any worry of humiliation, but at a high emotional cost.

No Particular Personality Type:

Furthermore, the fear of humiliation is not a special characteristic of any particular personality type. It is a normal emotion. No one can escape the terrible feelings associated with humiliation. A person cannot grow up without experiencing these feelings. However, some people suffer more in this area than others. The more one has suffered from humiliation the more one is prone to anger. This can be illustrated by the number of shootings in our schools by disgruntled students who, because they see themselves as outsiders, are driven by anger to retaliate and revenge. I always tell my patients that if and when they become angry for any reason, they should quickly search for the cause of this emotion by asking (1) "Is this anger necessary?" and (2) "Why do I make this situation or this person overly important to me?"

Structural Theory of Freud:

In addition to infantile narcissism, another of Sigmund Freud's contributions to psychoanalysis was to divide the person's mental structure into three parts. The first is the Id. This is for instincts that are unconscious and contains the two important drives, sexual and aggressive. The second structure is called the Ego, and it mainly deals with reality. The Ego is important for survival. Part of the Ego is conscious and part unconscious. It is a major source of defenses against the instinctual drives and necessary for functioning in everyday life. The third category is the Superego which functions as the conscience or moral force. The Superego's job is to balance out the other two agencies.

When a person is functioning well in life and society, the above three agencies are in harmony—each doing its job well. When a person is dysfunctional or has mental illness, it means that the three agencies (Id, Ego and Superego) are out of synchronization, and this causes chaos.

Theory—Emotion of Humiliation:

The emotion of humiliation is disturbing to most people, and millions suffer from this fear. This manifests itself in all kinds of neurotic behavior such as depression, social phobia, panic attacks, and the inability to find appropriate marriage partners. All of these symptoms are based on high sensitivity to humiliation that can cause withdrawal, anger and violence. For instance, as mentioned earlier, a driver who feels road rage when someone cuts in front of his car or the bully in the playground who gets pleasure humiliating other children are surprisingly sensitive to humiliation themselves. These acts of humiliating others are the result of prior experiences of humiliation and are caused by oversensitivity to humiliation and the need to discharge tension.

When the Id or instinctual drives system is too strong against the Ego and the Superego, we find psychosis or severe emotional illness. Psychosis prevents the person from dealing with reality. When the Superego is too strong, it could lead to inhibitions, physical symptoms or anxieties. If the Superego is too weak, it could lead to mental illness with no moral enforcer and lead to criminality of various types. For example, a weak Superego can result in psychopaths, sociopaths, and all kinds of criminal behavior. With the Ego, the story is completely different. The Ego can never be too strong or well functioning. When the Ego is doing its job well, the other two agencies are in synchronization and the person is functioning well. By reducing sensitivity to humiliation the ego strengthens automatically.

Reduce Suffering of Neurotics:

The hope in writing this book is to reduce the suffering of the average person with neurosis (defined as distorted thinking) who has a severe conscience or Superego and needs to strengthen the Ego in order to function better. In contrast, psychopaths and sociopaths need to strengthen their Superegos or consciences in order to function in a civilized society. Compared to neurotics, psychopaths and sociopaths are not overly affected by humiliation. People with poor consciences have trouble living in a civilized society because of lack of caring for others and other personality problems.

Power of Anger:

Furthermore, the power of anger caused by humiliation can lead to extreme violence against oneself or others. All those who kill or commit suicide are expressing anger on others or themselves. They want to show important people in their lives how they are suffering and expect others to also suffer. Those who use violence are sensitive to humiliation. When people are happy and more fulfilled they are less likely to suffer the humiliations that cause their desire for revenge.

Difference Between Cognitive Behavioral Therapy and Ego Psychology Therapy:

According to the American Heritage Dictionary the definition of cognitive behavioral therapy is as follows: "A highly structured psychotherapeutic method used to alter distorted attitudes and problem behavior by identifying and replacing negative inaccurate thoughts and changing the rewards for behaviors".

Thus Cognitive psychotherapy relies mainly on intellect and understanding what is happening in the present and tries to change distorted thinking and behavior by verbal exchange with the patient. Ego psychology also uses cognitive methodology such as intellect verbal suggestions and awareness of current functioning; however, there is a major difference between them. Ego psychology also includes understanding the unconscious processes as well. Ego psychology uses all the methods of Classical psychoanalytic therapy, including dream interpretation, unconscious wishes, and goes deeper into the patient's personality and unconscious and cognitive psychology. Ego psychology can now use suggestions in ego functioning such as reducing over-sensitivity to humiliation and embarrassment, as I recommend, which differs from Classical or Orthodox psychoanalysis. Ego psychology therapy also focuses on present-day functioning including defenses and intellectual understanding in addition to emotions or feelings. Cognitive psychotherapy avoids going into interpretation of the unconscious. While Ego psychotherapists must be psychoanalyzed themselves by other psychoanalysts in order to learn about their own unconscious and techniques for interpretation of the unconscious, cognitive therapists do not have to be psychoanalyzed. That in itself is a major difference. In my opinion, cognitive therapists only scratch the surface, which for some people may be enough. But for most patients, it is better to deal with the conscious and unconscious for lasting benefits.

TREATMENT AND PRACTICE:

Treating Anger:

Freud has pointed out that no one is normal. We all have at one time or another experienced depression, irrational fears, panic attacks, severe self-criticism, low self-esteem, personality disorders, anxiety, and so on. To some degree or another that is what life is all about. Therefore, because anger is important as "signal anger", psychologists, psychoanalysts or other members of the health provider community need to understand and deal with anger. I believe anger is the major cause of mental illness. I saw anger as important when working in a mental hospital and, furthermore, by just looking at the chaotic angry world we're living in. Based on the importance of anger, when I treat patients through interpretation I try to avoid criticizing the patient. For example, when an interpretation is made to a patient who feels criticized, the patient will feel humiliated and anger will follow. Whenever a patient gets angry it is linked to perception of being humiliated. The professionals must learn to recognize this behavior and learn how to deal with it.

Case History of Mr.Z:

For instance, in the psychoanalytic literature there is an interesting case written many years ago by Heinz Kohut. Kohut describes a Mr. Z who had had an unsuccessful treatment with a traditional classical psychoanalyst. Kohut treated this patient in a more sympathetic and empathic manner. I believe this reduced Mr. Z's fears of being humiliated thus allowing for a successful recovery.

Therefore, when treating my patients I have found that addressing their over-sensitivity to humiliation brings excellent results. If my patients can learn to reduce their sensitivity to humiliation, they usually provide many withheld ideas and fantasies. This freedom leads to improvement in their lives.

Case of Severe OCD (Obsessive-Compulsive Disorder):

The following is the case of a man in his 20s, a college graduate and very intelligent who came into therapy to deal with a case of OCD (obsessive-compulsive disorder). According to the Diagnostic and Statistical Manual DSM IV, OCD is described as follows: "The essential features of OCD are recurrent obsessions or compulsions—that are severe enough to be time-consuming (more than one hour per day) will cause marked distress or significant impairment. The disturbance is not due to direct physiological effects or of substance abuse. Obsessions are persistent ideas, thoughts, impulses or images that are experienced as intrusive and inappropriate and that cause marked anxiety or distress. The content of the obsessions is alien, not within his or her control and not the kind of thought that he or she would expect to have. Most common obsessions are repeated thoughts that are unacceptable. Compulsions are repeated behaviors (e.g., hand washing, constant checking, all mental acts such as praying, counting, repeating words silently), not to provide pleasure of all gratification. In most cases, the person feels driven to perform the compulsions to reduce the distress that accompanies an obsession or prevent some dreaded event or situation. The act or compulsion must cause marked distress, be time-consuming or significantly interfere with the individual's normal routine, occupation or usual social activities or relationships."

My patient's OCD was so severe he had to leave his job because it took him over three hours to shave in the morning, and thus he found it hard to leave his house for his job. His obsessions were also bothersome, and he suffered intensely. He did not realize that he was basically suffering from a severe Superego. He said his father was a control freak while his mother was extremely loving and solicitous.

This patient has a twin sister who is a beautiful woman happily married to a man similar in appearance to her brother but without the OCD, and has children. The patient says his father has OCD also but at a much lower degree and is a successful businessman. Again according to patient, the father's obsessions is money. His parents are now divorced.

The patient has had several other therapists of different types including a behaviorist and psychiatrists. He reported that his illness seemed to make his previous therapists nervous for unknown reasons and that I seemed very comfortable. He had tried medication in the past but it made him manic and frightened him. The previous therapists all agreed with the patient that his father was the main cause of his neurosis. My interpretations differed from them by indicating that the main problem was his difficulty in separating from his twin sister and his intense loneliness at the loss of her companionship. His obsessions were an attempt to deal with his feelings of loss of her because of her marriage and to defend against his loneliness. During treatment we worked to reduce his over-sensitivity to humiliation and embarrassment at his symptoms and the need for his sister. Interpretations to the effect that his behavior was normal under the circumstances of his loss caused him to be more relaxed. He was also struggling to maintain his own identity since his sister was so important to him over a long period of time while they were growing and developing. While it would have been better for him to have a more supportive father, his father was not the cause of his pathology.

After several months work at once or twice a week therapy, and with my urging him to reduce oversensitivity to humiliation and embarrassment as well as interpreting the need to reduce Superego severity, the patient was then able to look for a job and attain one in his field. He now seems well on the road to recovery. I maintain it was the reduction in over-sensitivity to humiliation and embarrassment that caused the change. The other important issues were his understanding how closeness to his twin sister and struggle for separate identity were his main problems.

Reducing Sensitivity to Humiliation:

As stated earlier, when I was in training to be a therapist the main focus was to reduce sensitivity to anxiety. Today I add humiliation to sensitivity reduction. My patients reduce sensitivity and fear of humiliation to help them understand the root of their problems. Indeed the main reason people do not take advantage of the process of psychotherapy is the fear of being humiliated. Anxiety is the fear of humiliation. This is because humiliation is the powerful inducer of negative feelings about the self. Since anxiety and humiliation are closely allied with annihilation or extinction, we can easily see why people avoid therapy if they expect pain.

Splitting of the Ego:

In addition, mental illness is seen in people who see things as black or white, good or bad with few shades of gray. This need to split thinking is based on the fear of humiliation or embarrassment. Such people cannot tolerate to be even a little wrong, and they deny or avoid contradiction in thinking and self-esteem. In treatment it is important to change this need to be rigid by appropriate psychoanalytic interpretations.

Making Unconscious Conscious:

In addition to Freud's Structural Theory (Id, Ego and Superego), his original idea to help patients was to make the unconscious (the part of the mental apparatus that is not available to the patient) conscious. In other words, the analyst's job was to interpret to the patient ideas and instincts that were repressed. With this information the patient was expected to make improvements. This did not work out entirely the way Freud had hoped. While most patients improved, some patients got better by what is known as the placebo effect. (The placebo's beneficial effect in a patient following a particular treatment arises from the patient's expectations concerning the treatment rather than from the treatment itself.) With some patients, the results of Freud's interpretations were not permanent and needed constant repetition. This often happens to many therapists.

Change in Procedure and Practice:

Today, practitioners of psychoanalysis since Freud have changed the therapeutic procedure. Instead of trying to make the unconscious conscious by interpretation, they focus on helping the Ego improve. They do this by improving the mental functions of the patient and by helping the patient adjust to reality. I propose that reducing over-sensitivity to humiliation and embarrassment will help the Ego improve more quickly and remain more permanent.

Insufficient Recognition of Importance of Humiliation:

As mentioned before, even though improving the Ego functioning has been helpful in many cases; I consider that the practitioners of psychoanalysis have insufficiently recognized the important emotion of humiliation. My main idea is that humiliation is important and central to the functioning by the Ego. All three mental agencies described above, Ego, Id and Superego, depend on reduced sensitivity to humiliation to function well. With oversensitivity to humiliation, the Ego and Id become inhibited. If sensitivity to humiliation is overly relaxed, distortions of judgment by the Superego could lead to criminality. It is important to get the right amount of sensitivity to humiliation in order to help people return to mental health and a satisfied life. This comes about by reducing over-sensitivity to humiliation and embarrassment and thus helping the Ego develop and improve reality testing and functioning in everyday life.

Trace Humiliation from Past to Present:

In other words, the main procedure for psychoanalysts today is to deal with the patient's feelings in the present and the past and to understand the effect of the past in the present. In addition to understanding the past, my therapeutic work traces the history of humiliation from the past to the present. We then get the opportunity to improve the emotional functioning. For example, if the patient experiences anger at the therapist too often or too easily, the original anger and humiliation probably happened in the past frequently with parental figures. There is reason to believe that angry feelings come from early humiliation in the patient's history and are continuing to the present.

When the analyst can interpret and encourage the patient to reduce sensitivity to humiliation, the patient will make remarkable progress, because humiliation is one of the most powerful emotions.

Therapeutic Procedure:

Thus, when working with a patient and the speaking process starts to slow down, I have found that this is the time to introduce the notion of sensitivity to humiliation or embarrassment. We discuss how sensitivity to humiliation and embarrassment might affect the patient's freedom to express themselves. Usually this approach leads to a breakthrough. In addition to the benefit of allowing the patient to speak more freely in the session, we now know the reason for any anger in my office or anywhere else. This is recognized by the patient as humiliation.

Two main ideas in therapy:

In addition to allowing the patient to speak more freely in the session, there are two main ideas that I transmit to patients when they feel anger. (1). Either they are being overly sensitive to humiliation or (2).For some unknown reason they are giving the humiliator's ideas or existence too much importance. We then search for explanations why the person who humiliates is held in such high esteem. This discussion leads to important insight, changes behavior, and reduces the feeling of anger. The main idea is to teach the patient to associate anger with humiliation so as to be able to quickly locate the real problem.

Anger at the Therapist:

Therefore, when the patient is angry with the therapist, the search for the cause is initiated. The patient is under the threat of humiliation by some idea or fantasy that causes the withholding of speech, and quite often the patient attempts to try to humiliate the therapist. The patient might make reference to something wrong with the office, or the dress of the therapist, or make some negative remarks about what is happening in the treatment. They may claim to be over-charged or complain that they are not getting better faster. It is at this time, that the therapist can ask if the patient is trying to humiliate the therapist, and together they search for the cause. Thus, once a therapist understands that the need of the patient to criticize is based on the patient over-sensitivity to humiliation, there is no need for the therapist to become defensive. Instead it is welcomed, because this means the therapy is getting closer to what is bothering the patient, especially in terms of content that provokes humiliation. This can lead to important material and insights to the patient's problems. In this way patients can become free to express their fantasies and fears as they relate to the therapist.

Trace the Anger:

Therefore, after learning how to trace the cause of anger by looking for humiliation, therapy begins to have a positive effect. The patient becomes happier, more productive, and feels joy. The reason for increase of pleasure comes from decrease of anger and less fear of humiliation. There is also a reduction of the criticizing Superego or conscience and an increase in the sense of the power to do what is important and healthy without overly worrying what others might think.

<u>Case History of Mr. X:</u>

An example of a patients' response to reducing over-sensitivity to humiliation is the case of Mr. X. who was 20 years old when he first came to treatment. He presented problems of general unhappiness, anger, physical difficulties of all kinds, including asthma, coughing, and trouble relating to women. He also had difficulty in completing school assignments. His problems began shortly after birth when he and his mother were forced to live in a hospital during wartime where she worked at a non-professional job. Also, his father was away in the army. The mother could not give the patient the full attention every new-born needs. This was the first humiliation. In addition, after the war the parents were dysfunctional as a couple.

When he first started treatment, Mr. X had neurotic symptoms of various types such as poor self-esteem, anger and frustration. He also had physical symptoms including asthma, coughing and mild depressive episodes. In addition he had problems relating to women.

The patient took to treatment easily because he realized he needed help to accomplish what he wanted. Both his parents were professionals and were supportive of his desire for help. He did have a previous therapist but was frightened of her because she was too permissive. This was interpreted by his unconscious psyche as seduction.

When I first started treatment with Mr. X, I was a traditional classical analyst and had not discovered the importance of over-sensitivity to humiliation. Even so, in time Mr. X's symptoms were reduced, as evidence by the fact that he had a girlfriend. However without consulting me and during the summer vacation, the patient married his girlfriend and it turned out to be difficult relationship. The result was she left him for another man, which devastated my patient. For a long period of time the patient was frustrated by his difficulty in connecting to another woman and was also plagued by doubts of his manhood.

During this period when the patient was suffering he expressed much anger at his condition of loneliness. At this time, I came upon the idea and importance of the feelings of humiliation. This was based on the patient's associations and behavior. In addition, the patient was always trying to humiliate me for not helping him with his problems fast enough. I realized then that the patient was suffering from humiliation. It was only after an interpretation made to him to the effect that he was "oversensitive to humiliation and must reduce this sensitivity" that he was able to relax and enjoy the search for a new partner in life. He made good progress in therapy, found a suitable partner and now has his own family.

Case History of Agoraphobia:

In another case, a patient of mine had a severe case of agoraphobia (fear of open spaces). Unfortunately, he needed to cross the Atlantic Ocean to relocate with his British wife. He came to therapy to overcome this fear of leaving home, and after several sessions we were able to discover a severe embarrassment and humiliation he suffered as a teenager. This memory and discussion led to a reduction in his sensitivity to humiliation. A joyful letter from him after his successful trip expressed gratitude for our work together.

Need for Repetition:

There is an old saying that "repetition is the best way to learn something." This is certainly true in psychological treatment. Repetition of good experiences is necessary to make changes in responding to anger and humiliation. By giving up old responses and reducing over-sensitivity to humiliation, people feel in control of their lives and feel more power.

Humiliation Must be Reduced:

Hence, in order to allow people more freedom to pursue worthy goals and achieve success, the power of the "H" word must be lessened. Reducing over-sensitivity to humiliation or fear of humiliation can also lead to more joy and happiness because it reduces anger and rage. Although everyone has experienced humiliation that leads to anger, the extent and intensity of these angry feelings have been seldom appreciated or understood.

Sensitivity to Humiliation Reduced by Treatment:

Thus, as mentioned earlier, when a person is over-sensitive to humiliation and embarrassment, it is difficult to be happy. The reason for this difficulty is seen in heightened alertness to danger and the need to keep defenses on the ready. With this condition of high alert, one cannot relax and is ready to pounce on any person or situation that is potentially hurtful. The fear of being hurt is real to the humility-sensitive person because it is experienced as belittlement or, even worse, annihilation. The fear of extinction is very painful and triggers anger in order to ward off the attack. Most likely, sensitivity to humiliation is connected to any anxiety that people might feel. I have found that fear of humiliation is a factor in all mental problems because it leads to the need for more and more defenses or protections against anxiety. The more defenses you have, the more baggage you carry. This leads to mental distortions in order to function. These distortions are the major causes of mental problems because they interfere with reality.

Practice of Therapy:

Therefore, as a psychologist I have discovered that it is important to preface any interpretation to a patient with "Try not to take these words as a criticism." Such language usually helps my patients deal with the new information without their getting angry. Long before we can interpret the patient's behavior and verbal associations or words, we have to encourage the reduction of sensitivity to humiliation. When this is accomplished, therapy proceeds along expected lines.

Looking Back at Practice in 600 School:

Looking back, if I was now working in the "600 schools" that I mentioned earlier, where emotionally disturbed boys were continually angry, I would now teach reducing sensitivity to humiliation. Anger should be recognized as the first response to humiliation. This would not be a program of anger management, but anger understanding and reduction based on my recognition of the importance of over-sensitivity to humiliation.

4

CONQUERING HUMILIATION

In this chapter I will discuss how to overcome and conquer humiliation and embarrassment. The issues to be resolved are (1).How to recognize humiliation and embarrassment. (2).The problems that may impede or hinder discovery or recognition of humiliation and embarrassment. (3).The actual method of reduction of sensitivity to humiliation and embarrassment.

Anger and humiliation go together, conquer one and you have conquered the other. The process of change is difficult, but even surface help can sometimes be better than no help at all. Recognizing the problem is the first step towards solving the problem.

Recognition:

How can you recognize the level of sensitivity to humiliation in your life? The first clue is anger. Remember, anger and humiliation always goes together. Whenever you feel anger, there is sure to be underlying humiliation. The level of sensitivity to humiliation is based on how easily you are angered. But what is the underlying humiliation? The next time you feel anger, look at it closely. What was the "trigger?" It must be humiliation if you respond with anger. When you are overly-sensitive to humiliation this anger can be followed by aggression, violence, and the feeling of wanting to get even. Since you are probably not psychopathic, you will naturally try to avoid violence and aggression. But maybe you think about getting even? Do you come up with a "clever" remark or perhaps a "put down?" Look for the humiliation behind the anger, and the anger from humiliation. This is a new concept and takes some time to learn and apply. It might be easier to look at others. For example, if you are late for a dinner, your partner may be furious. Why? Your lateness is felt by the other as belittling, ignoring, not validating, in other words, humiliating.

Problem with Locating Source of Anger:

Whenever a person is unable to locate the reason for the anger, the cause of the anger can be unknown or unconscious. An analogy often given in psychology of the explanation of unconscious is in the description of an iceberg. The part of the iceberg seen is the conscious and the part under water is the unconscious. In reality the part of the iceberg underwater is much larger than the part above. The same applies to the Conscious which is much smaller in many different ways than the Unconscious. Anger, when the reason cannot be located, is often turned inward and you feel criticized and even depressed. At this time it is important to seek professional help.

Problem of Psychic Reality:

However, the real problem in dealing with humiliation and embarrassment is the complicated nature of every individual person's psychic reality. Psychic reality means that each person interprets the events, situations and fantasies in his or her own particular point of view. When psychic reality is distorted, it causes problems either benign or severe. Everyone has a view of life based on this mind set; this is known as psychic reality. The job of the therapists is to help improve the psychic reality of patients as it effects the present functioning. For example, a man may blame his wife for his problems. In reality she may have little or nothing to do with his problem or the situation. The blaming of others for one's own troubles is caused by this inner view of distorted reality. With reduced sensitivity to humiliation one learns that no one is perfect.

Reduction of Sensitivity to Humiliation and Anger:

Thus, after recognizing the source of the humiliation and anger and overcoming the specific pertinent issues, the next step is to learn how to reduce the over-sensitivity to humiliation and embarrassment. The question is <u>how</u> to reduce this fear of humiliation and embarrassment? As in all things, for some people it is easy and for others it can be a difficult procedure. The first and most important step in reduction of oversensitivity to humiliation is to be aware of any feelings of anger. Instead of reacting to anger, one must say to self "Where does this humiliation come from?" The next step is to search for the cause, and avoid immediate, perhaps inappropriate action. Once the cause of the underlying humiliation is located, then look closely at the present angering situation. Ask yourself, "Could I be making the person who is causing my anger overly important?" For example: While driving a car, another driver cuts in front. If you get angry you are automatically making this driver important to you. Why should you make this person important? He or she means nothing to you. However, whenever you are feeling anger toward a family member the situation is not so clear because that person *is* important. Therefore, when searching for humiliation the emphasis has to be not only on the situation but also on the individuals involved.

When we feel anger toward another we should become aware that we are making the other person too important. The threat of humiliation is then reduced or eliminated. We no longer need the defensive mode. In other words we do not need to get angry and react.

Guidelines for Reducing Oversensitivity:

Specifically, how can someone on his or her own reduce sensitivity to humiliation and embarrassment? Below are some guidelines.

(1).Whenever anger is felt do not act or react

(2).Search for the cause of the humiliation

(3).After locating the present cause of humiliation, ask, "Why am I making this person or event so important to me?"

(4).If you cannot locate the cause of humiliation or embarrassment, say to yourself, "The cause will be found in time and in the meantime cool it."

(5).Eventually, with effort the cause of anger will be found, but in the meantime do not over-react.

(6). If the cause is not found and anger persists, look for a name of a psychotherapist, preferably someone trained in psychoanalysis and who understands the importance of humiliation. In the meantime, try on your own steps 1-5 to reduce over-sensitivity to humiliation or embarrassment.

(7).Even if you do not find the cause of the anger or the humiliation behind it, by thinking instead of action you are automatically improving your ego functioning. Good ego functioning is important for mental health.

5

CONCLUSION

Why I Wrote This Book:

As stated throughout, I wrote this book to help people live a more joyful life, to be less neurotic, and to overcome fears of all kinds. With less social anxiety (discomfort with people), social phobia disappears. People put less blame on partners, husbands, wives, mothers, fathers, siblings, and others so that relationships can improve. In fact, there is less fear of others. For example, a shopper who once had a hard time saying "no" or asking for a lower price can finally do so without anxiety. A healthy person can be less concerned what unimportant people think of them and can be themselves under all conditions.

Reason for Hate and Violence:

The reason people hate, attack, and destroy their fellow human beings is the result of conscious or unconscious humiliations experienced during early childhood development. Thus childhood experiences of humiliation and embarrassment caused by parental, cultural, economic, or other forces produce anger that is often repeated. Anger turned outward leads to social unrest and violence, while anger turned inward can lead to depression and suicide.

Mental Illness:

Furthermore, my theory of "over-sensitivity to humiliation" goes beyond just understanding personal and global fears. I believe that fear of intense humiliation may be the underlying cause of serious mental illness. Hate and anger do not allow for feelings of love. Love brings people together. Anger and hate drive people apart. Only the mentally healthy can love. Love can only be accomplished by reducing over-sensitivity to humiliation to a minimum.

Alertness to Danger:

Thus when a person is over-sensitive to humiliation it is difficult to be happy. The reason for this difficulty is seen in his or her heightened alertness to danger and the need to keep defenses at the ready. With this condition of high alert, one cannot relax and is ready to pounce on any situation that is seen as potentially hurtful. The fear of being hurt is real to the overly-sensitive person because it is experienced as belittlement, or, even worse, annihilation. The fear of extinction is painful and causes anger to ward off a potential attack.

Avoidance of Psychotherapy:

Everyone has problems, and I have found that the main reason people avoid getting help is fear of humiliation. Most relatively healthy people can deal with humiliation to a limited extent and accept help from an outsider trained in the process. Therefore, in general when you are unable to reduce oversensitivity to humiliation by working on it alone professional help is needed. However, try to choose a therapist who is aware of the importance of humiliation in therapy.

Goal of Life:

Nevertheless, from time to time there are people who come for therapy with problems that at first seen unrelated to humiliation. In addition, these people have trouble expressing their ideas and feelings. By reducing fear of humiliation and embarrassment, they are able to make major changes in ability to speak of problems and then make changes in life to be happy. As Reuben Fine, referred to earlier, wrote in his book The Healing of the Mind, "Happiness is one of the major goals of psychotherapy." I have found that the importance of reducing over-sensitivity to humiliation cannot be overstated, for anger is caused by humiliation, and anger keeps one from being happy.

Summary:

To summarize, once you lose sensitivity to humiliation, the fear of extinction or annihilation is reduced, and the need for high protection is gone. Joy and happiness is accomplished through relaxation and loss of fear. My discovery of the importance of humiliation has helped my patients to understand their own anger and how to reduce it. Reducing oversensitivity to humiliation has improved their lives enormously. My recognition of the concept of reducing sensitivity to humiliation and embarrassment has been revolutionary in helping my patients deal with other people and reality. Recognizing the power of humiliation—dreaded "H" word—is ground-breaking as both a concept and in the development of new treatment methods.

BIBLIOGRAPHY

Blanck, Gertrude & Blanck, Rubin (1986): Beyond Ego Psychology: New York: Columbia University Press

Buetens, Bernard R. (1974): The Comparative Effects of Affection and Hostility in Reducing Frustration Induced Anger Among Delinquents and Non-delinquents: Ph.D Dissertation: New York University

Dollard, J., & Miller, N.E., (1939): Frustration and Aggression. New Haven: Yale University Press

Fine, Reuben (1985): The Meaning of Love in Human Experience: New York: John Wiley and Sons

Fine, Reuben (1982): The Healing of the Mind: (2nd Edition): New York: Columbia University Press

Freud, Sigmund (1901-05): The Standard Edition: Volume VII: Fragment of an Analysis of a Case of Hysteria: London: The Hogarth Press and The Institute of Psychoanalysis

Friedman, Thomas (2003): The Humiliation Factor: NY Times: Op Ed. Nov. 9, 2003

Goleman, Daniel (1995): Emotional Intelligence: New York: Bantam Books

Kohut, Heinz (1980): Advances in Self Psychology: pg 449: New York: International University Press, Inc.

Moore, B.E., & Fine, B. D., (1990): Psychoanalytic Terms and Concepts: New Haven & London: The American Psychoanalytic Association & Yale U. Press

Turow, Scott (1977): One L: The Turbulent True Story of a First Year at Harvard Law School: New York: Putnam

ABOUT THE AUTHOR

Bernard R. Buetens is a psychoanalyst in private practice with a Ph.D. from New York University, a Master of Arts degree from Columbia University, and a graduate of Washington Square Psychotherapy Institute in New York City. Dr. Buetens has been a Psychologist and Psychoanalytic Psychotherapist in private practice for over 30 years in the New York metropolitan area.

INDEX

978-0-595-37916-3
0-595-37916-8